D1536137

WITHDRAWN

Japanese Americans

SPIRIT
of America®

Japanese AMERICANS

By Melissa McDaniel

The Child's World®
Chanhassen, Minnesota

Japanese AMERICANS

Published in the United States of America by The Child's World®
PO Box 326 • Chanhassen, MN 55317-0326 • 800-599-READ • www.childsworld.com

Acknowledgments
   The Child's World®: Mary Berendes, Publishing Director

   Editorial Directions, Inc.: E. Russell Primm, Emily Dolbear, Sarah E. De Capua, and Lucia Raatma, Editors; Linda S. Koutris, Photo
   Selector; Image Select International, Photo Research; Red Line Editorial and Pam Rosenberg, Fact Research; Tim Griffin/IndexServ,
   Indexer; Donna Frassetto, Proofreader

Photos
   Cover/frontispiece: A Japanese-American inductee into the volunteer combat regiment posing with his family in Kauai, Hawaii, in 1943

   Cover photographs ©: Library of Congress; PictureQuest

   Interior photographs ©: Getty Image, 6, 7; AKG-Images, Berlin, 8 top, 8 bottom, 9; 10 Corbis; 11, AKG-Images, Berlin, 11; Library
   of Congress, 12, 13, 14; Corbis, 15; Getty Images, 16; Library of Congress, 17; Getty Images, 18 top, Library of Congress, 18 bottom;
   U.S. Army Centre of Military History, 19; Getty Images, 20; TRIP, 21; Corbis, 23, 24, 25 top, 25 bottom, 26 top, 26 bottom; Getty
   Images/Photodisc, 27 top; 27 bottom; Corbis, 28.

Registration
   The Child's World®, Spirit of America®, and their associated logos are the sole property and
   registered trademarks of The Child's World®.

Library of Congress Cataloging-in-Publication Data
   McDaniel, Melissa.
    Japanese Americans / by Melissa McDaniel.
       p. cm.
   "Spirit of America."
   Includes index.
   Summary: Brief introduction to the history, heritage, culture, and
   customs of Japanese Americans.
    ISBN 1-56766-154-8 (lib. bound : alk. paper)
    1. Japanese Americans—Juvenile literature. [1. Japanese Americans.]
   I. Title.
    E184.J3 M43 2002
    305.895'6073—dc21
                                    2001008616

Contents

Chapter ONE

Leaving Home

Three Japanese samurai, warriors known for their courage and loyalty

FEW IMMIGRANT GROUPS IN AMERICA HAVE had to face the official **discrimination** that the Japanese have endured. In spite of this, however, Japanese people have achieved great success in America.

Japan is a string of islands off the east coast of mainland Asia. These islands are covered with mountains. For centuries, many Japanese people farmed the mountain slopes for a living. Other Japanese were *samurai*, warriors famed for their courage and loyalty. Centuries of **tradition** controlled Japanese culture.

There was a right way to do everything. Even the tea ceremony had specific rules.

Starting in the 1600s, Japan cut itself off from the rest of the world. Japan's leaders did not want the outside world to change Japan, so they closed Japanese ports to ships

In the mid-1800s, Commodore Matthew C. Perry landed at this spot in Tokyo Bay.

from other nations. They also refused to let Japanese people travel to foreign lands.

All of this began to change in 1853, when Commodore Matthew C. Perry of the U.S. Navy sailed into Tokyo Harbor. He convinced the Japanese leaders to allow trade with outsiders.

In the years following Perry's visit, Japan changed quickly. An emperor named Mutsuhito, adopted *Meiji*, meaning "enlightened rule," as the name for the era of his reign. He was

Emperor Mutsuhito and his family

Hundreds of Japanese immigrants arriving on the West Coast

in power from 1868 to 1912, a span of time known as the Meiji era. Mutsuhito recognized that Japan's **isolation** from the rest of the world had made the country fall behind other nations. He wanted to make Japan's military forces stronger and help its industries grow. To do this, the government needed money. It started placing high taxes on farmers. Many farmers could not afford to pay the taxes, and more than 300,000 farmers lost their land as a result. This was the start of a moving *netsu*, or fever. Suddenly, thousands of young men wanted to leave Japan. In 1885, the Japanese government finally started letting people travel

8

outside the country. In the next 40 years, about 380,000 Japanese would move to Hawaii and the West Coast of the United States.

Many wanted to work hard for a few years and earn a lot of money. Then they planned to return to Japan and buy back the farms they had lost or pay off the debts they owed. In a country where honor and duty are among the highest values, this was believed to be the honorable thing to do.

Troops arriving during the 1905 war between Japan and Russia

Other Japanese planned to leave the country permanently. In 1905, a war started between Japan and Russia. Many young men who did not want to fight in the war chose instead to make a new life for themselves in the United States. Still others were simply trying to get away from the many rules that governed life in Japan.

9

In 1885, the U.S government said that it was looking for 600 people to work in Hawaii. The government then received 28,000 applications from citizens eager to leave Japan.

Officials examining the documents of Japanese women trying to enter the United States

The huge flow of Japanese immigrants to Hawaii and to America's West Coast ended suddenly. In 1908, an agreement between the United States and Japan stopped workers from moving to America. But it allowed the parents, wives, and children of people who were already living in the United States to join them. In the next few years, tens of thousands of Japanese women entered the United States. Many were joining their husbands. Some, however, **forged** official-looking documents to enter the United States.

In 1924, racism and fear of outsiders led the U.S. Congress to pass a law ending all immigration from Japan. By this time, 250,000 Japanese people were living in the United States.

TRADITIONALLY IN JAPAN, YOUNG PEOPLE DID NOT CHOOSE their own marriage partners. Instead, parents arranged marriages for their children, based upon what would be best for the families. Often, the couple would trade pictures before they met for the first time.

Japanese immigrants to America continued to follow this custom. A man who wanted a wife sent his picture to Japan. Then someone in Japan would send him pictures of Japanese women who were looking for a husband. The immigrant would choose his wife from among those pictures. The woman he selected sailed for the United States, never having met her husband. She was often quite surprised when she saw him at the dock. Usually, he was much older than his picture and much poorer than he had claimed to be. But they were already considered married, so she could not go back home. About 20,000 Japanese women came to the United States as "picture brides" (above).

11

Chapter Two

Hard Times

Japanese Americans working on a sugar beet farm in Oregon

LIFE IN THE UNITED STATES WAS NOT AS EASY as Japanese immigrants had hoped. Many who settled in Hawaii had agreed to work on sugar plantations for three years. This work was much more difficult than they had expected. A siren blared every morning at five o'clock, waking the workers. Some went off to the fields to hoe weeds or cut sugarcane. Others went to hot, noisy factories where the sugarcane was turned into sugar. Either way, it was hard, miserable work.

Often, the Japanese workers endured harsh treatment. Sometimes their bosses hit them. They were also given identification numbers. The bosses called out these numbers rather than using their names.

Over time, life in the Hawaiian Islands improved for the Japanese. They banded together to demand better wages. They started families and decided not to return to Japan. They opened their own businesses and became part of the mainstream of Hawaiian life. By the 1920s, 43 percent of the people in Hawaii were of Japanese ancestry.

Japanese-American children also helped out with the farm work.

Japanese immigrants in the mainland United States had a more difficult time, however. At first, most Issei who settled on the West Coast worked on farms. Others found jobs in hotels, **sawmills**, and small stores. As they saved money, they began opening their own stores and buying farmland. Some became successful farmers. This made many other Californians nervous. They believed all of California's available land would be bought by the Japanese. In 1913,

Interesting Fact

Each generation of Japanese Americans has a special name. Japanese immigrants are called *Issei*. Their children, who were born in the United States, are called *Nisei*. The children of Nisei are called *Sansei*. And the children of Sansei are called *Yonsei*.

The neighborhood of Little Tokyo in Los Angeles, California, in 1942

the state responded by passing a law that kept Japanese immigrants from buying land.

Japanese farmers, however, found ways around this law. Some bought land in the names of their children, who had been born in the United States. Others formed corporations to buy the land. A second law, which went into effect in 1920, put an end to these practices. Now, Issei could not even rent land. All they could do was ask friendly whites to rent or buy the land for them.

Japanese Americans on the West Coast often faced discrimination everywhere they went. Many white Americans did not want them living in their neighborhood or going to school with their children. Many barbers refused to cut Japanese hair. Movie theaters often seated Japanese people in separate sections.

14

Rejected by American society, Japanese Americans took care of themselves. They shopped in their own stores, ate in their own restaurants, and borrowed money from their own banks. The neighborhoods where Japanese Americans lived and worked were known as Little Tokyos, after the capital of Japan. Little Tokyos thrived in cities up and down the West Coast.

The Issei thought a good education would help their children rise above the discrimination. So Nisei children studied hard and got good grades. Many went to college. But when they finished college, they found that white businesses would not hire them. Nisei engineers and accountants had no choice but to work in the same small shops as their parents. By 1940, however, more than half

A Japanese-American cleaning store in Little Tokyo, proud to display its American patriotism

the Japanese Americans on the West Coast worked in their own businesses! Only 5 percent worked in businesses owned by whites.

But for Japanese Americans in the United States, the worst was yet to come. As the 1940s began, World War II (1939–1945) was already raging in Europe and Asia. Then, on December 7, 1941, Japan bombed the U.S. Naval Base at Pearl Harbor, Hawaii. The Japanese bombed the base hoping to draw the United States into the war. The next day, the United States declared war on Japan. As a result of the shock and **resentment** caused by the bombing, many Americans became suspicious of anyone of Japanese ancestry.

The U.S.S. Arizona *on fire after the Japanese attack on Pearl Harbor on December 7, 1941*

In February 1942, President Franklin Delano Roosevelt ordered that people of Japanese descent living on the West Coast be sent to **internment camps** farther inland. It did not matter whether they were men, women, or children, Issei or Nisei,

U.S. citizens or not. Nor did it matter that most had never shown any sign of being disloyal to the United States. A total of 120,000 Japanese Americans were relocated to internment camps.

In a short period of time—in some cases, just a few days—Japanese Americans had to figure out what to do with their houses and land. Some sold their land for only a fraction of what it was worth. Others simply locked their doors and hoped that everything would still be there when they got back.

This Japanese family is waiting to be taken to an internment camp in April 1942.

The internment camps were a lot like prisons. Barbed-wire fences surrounded the area, and armed guards made sure nobody left the camps. Inside, families did their best to improve their surroundings. They hung curtains and put up colorful posters and calendars. Many made paper flowers to add still more color to their small space. Adults in the camps worked long hours for little pay as teachers in the schools they had set up. They

Soldiers as well as Japanese-American citizens at an internment camp in Manzar, California

Many young Japanese-American men were eager to serve in the U.S. armed forces during World War II.

also worked as doctors and nurses in the camp hospitals. They were not allowed to run private businesses, so they set up **cooperatives**. The cooperatives provided goods, such as food items and household supplies, and services, such as beauty parlors.

Meanwhile, Japanese Americans in Hawaii lived their lives normally. Perhaps they were not sent to camps because such a high percentage of Hawaiians were of Japanese ancestry. And they were just too important to life there. Only on the mainland, where Japanese Americans were seen as outsiders, were they sent away.

In time, some Japanese Americans were allowed to leave the camps to join the U.S. Army. Others were allowed to leave for college. Then, in 1944, the Supreme Court of the United States ruled that imprisoning Japanese Americans without just cause was illegal. The camps were shut down, and Japanese Americans headed home to try to put the pieces of their lives back together.

DURING WORLD WAR II, Japanese Americans were as eager to fight for their country as other Americans. Many Hawaiians and some mainlanders who had been released from the camps joined the 442nd Regimental Combat Team (left). These soldiers fought many bloody battles in Italy. They proved to be among the toughest, bravest soldiers in the army. Shig Doi went to Europe with 990 other soldiers in the 442nd. "Just think," he said, "not more than 200 of them came back without getting hit."

In all, the men of the 442nd earned more than 18,000 individual military honors. The 442nd is believed to have received more honors than any other unit in U.S. military history.

Chapter THREE

Starting Over

Daniel K. Inouye of Hawaii, the first Japanese American to be elected to the U.S. Senate

IN SOME PARTS OF AMERICA, Japanese Americans were welcomed back warmly by their neighbors. In others, discrimination was as strong as ever. Some Japanese Americans returned home to find that their houses had been vandalized or allowed to fall into ruins. Many people never got back the land they had been forced to leave. They had to start over.

Much legal discrimination against Japanese Americans ended in the years after World War II. Laws were changed so that Japanese people could once again immigrate to the United States. Nonwhite immigrants who had been barred from becoming U.S. citizens were finally allowed to seek citizenship. Many Issei rushed to become citizens.

Japanese Americans took another big step forward in 1959, when Hawaii became the 50th state in the Union. Japanese Americans began to hold important jobs in government. Daniel Inouye and Spark Matsunaga were the first Japanese Americans to win seats in the U.S. Senate.

Japanese Americans now hold jobs in all kinds of businesses.

As time went on, more and more Nisei and Sansei began to attend college. Doors that had been closed to their parents were open to them. Many Japanese Americans became doctors, scientists, and businesspeople. As they found success, many moved into **suburbs**. Today, most

Japanese Americans have blended into American society. Los Angeles, California, is one of the few West Coast cities that still has a Little Tokyo.

For many years, most Issei and Nisei who had been sent to the internment camps refused to talk about their experiences. They were ashamed of what had happened to them. But their children wanted to know. So, over time, more and more Japanese Americans began speaking out. They demanded that the U.S. government officially apologize for the internment. They also pressured the government to pay them money to make up for the damage that had been done to them.

In 1988, the U.S. Congress passed a law apologizing for the internment. The law gave $20,000 to each person who had spent time in the camps. This money was supposed to make up for the land, belongings, and wages Japanese Americans had lost during the war. But it did not come close to making up for the emotional pain that Japanese Americans suffered during their internment. However, it helped them to know that the government was finally willing to accept responsibility for what it had done to them.

*A Japanese-American woman, still
proud of her adopted home, sewing an
American flag during World War II*

Chapter FOUR

Grace and Beauty

Kristi Yamaguchi, winner of a 1992 Olympic gold medal

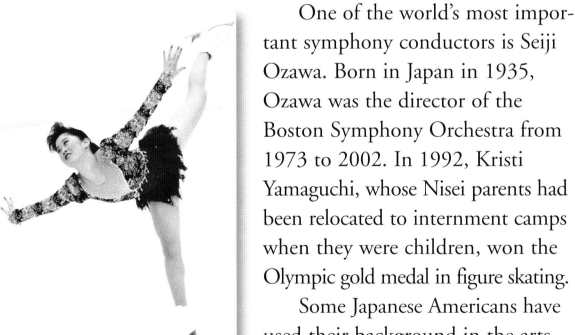

FOR DECADES, JAPANESE AMERICANS WERE held back by discrimination. Like many other immigrant groups, though, most Japanese Americans persevered and became successful.

One of the world's most important symphony conductors is Seiji Ozawa. Born in Japan in 1935, Ozawa was the director of the Boston Symphony Orchestra from 1973 to 2002. In 1992, Kristi Yamaguchi, whose Nisei parents had been relocated to internment camps when they were children, won the Olympic gold medal in figure skating.

Some Japanese Americans have used their background in the arts. Writers such as Lydia Minatoya,

David Mura, and Kyoko Mori have written about moving back and forth between Japanese and American cultures. Artist Isamu Noguchi became famous for his **abstract** sculptures. Noguchi's art is graceful and balanced. In this, it was influenced by Japanese art.

Sculptor Isamu Noguchi is known for his abstract work.

Other Japanese-Americans have demonstrated their talent as actors and actresses in television and film. Noriyuki "Pat" Morita is well-known for his role as Arnold on the television show *Happy Days* as well as for playing the the intelligent teacher in The *Karate Kid* films. More recently, Japanese-American Dean Cain portrayed Superman on the television's hit show *Lois and Clark*.

Dean Cain made a name for himself as Superman on television's Lois and Clark.

Americans have taken parts of Japanese culture to heart. Many people admire the grace and beauty of the **haiku**. This short poem consists of three lines. The first line has five syllables. The second line has seven syllables. The third line has five syllables, like the first line. Nature and the seasons are usually the subjects of the haiku.

Ellison Onizuka, the first Japanese American in space

Here is an example by Issa, who lived from 1762 to 1826.

A giant firefly:
that way, this way, that way, this—
and it passes by.

Ellison Onizuka was the first Japanese American in space. He was born in Hawaii, the grandson of Japanese immigrants who worked on Hawaiian sugar plantations. He joined the U.S. astronaut program in 1978, but his career was cut tragically short. He was killed in the 1986 *Challenger* explosion.

Japanese martial arts such as judo and karate are quite popular in the United States. A lot of people enjoy singing along to their

Americans of all backgrounds enjoy practicing Japanese martial arts.

favorite song at a **karaoke** machine. Even Japanese cartoons, comic books, and video games have influenced American style.

Many Americans, no matter what their ethnic background, enjoy a meal of traditional Japanese food. Tempura—deep-fried vegetables or shrimp—is a popular dish. Another favorite is soup filled with thick, chewy udon noodles. But many people's best-loved Japanese food is sushi. This is made of cold rice formed into a variety of shapes and served with raw fish or shellfish.

Japanese Americans have made numerous contributions to American society and culture. The United States is surely a richer place as a result.

Sushi is one of the most popular dishes in Japanese restaurants.

ONE OF THE WAYS JAPANESE AMERICANS CAN KEEP IN TOUCH WITH THEIR history is by celebrating Japanese holidays. Two of the most popular are Boys' Day and Girls' Day. Boys' Day—May 5—honors sons. On this day, families fly carp flags outside their houses. The carp symbolizes courage. On Girls' Day—March 3—young girls dress up in traditional clothing, visit friends, and hold tea parties.

1853 Commodore Matthew C. Perry of the U.S. Navy sails into Tokyo Harbor.

1885 The Japanese government begins allowing people to travel outside the country.

1905 War breaks out between Russia and Japan; many Japanese seek to avoid fighting by moving to the U.S.

1908 The U.S. reaches an agreement with Japan that stops Japanese workers from moving to America; the agreement does allow parents, wives and children of those already living in the U.S. to join them.

1913 The state of California passes a law that bars Japanese immigrants from buying land.

1924 The U.S. Congress passes a law ending all immigration from Japan.

1941 The Japanese bomb the U.S. Naval Base at Pearl Harbor, Hawaii, on December 7th.

1942 President Franklin D. Roosevelt orders all people of Japanese descent living on the West Coast to be sent to internment camps.

1944 The U.S. Supreme Court rules that internment of Japanese is illegal and those in internment camps are allowed to return to their homes.

1959 Hawaii becomes the 50th state of the Union.

1962 Daniel K. Inouye of Hawaii becomes the first Japanese American to be elected to the U.S. Senate.

1986 Japanese American astronaut Ellison Onizuka dies in the *Challenger* disaster.

1988 The U.S. Congress passes a law apologizing for the internment of Japanese during World War II and gives a monetary settlement to each person who spent time in the camps.

1992 Kristi Yamaguchi wins a gold medal in figure skating at the Winter Olympics in Albertville, France.

abstract (AB-strakt)
Art that is abstract has a general form and does not attempt to represent a picture or story in any obvious way. Isamu Noguchi was known for his abstract sculptures.

cooperatives (ko-AHP-uh-ruht-ivs)
Cooperatives are associations that form to allow their members to buy and sell things at better prices. Japanese Americans set up cooperatives within the internment camps.

discrimination (dis-krim-ih-NAY-shun)
Discrimination is the unfair treatment of a group of people because of their race or background. The Japanese faced discrimination for many years in the United States.

forged (FORJD)
Something that is forged has been faked, and it is not real. Some Japanese immigrants forged documents to gain entrance to the United States.

haiku (HI-koo)
Haiku is a type of poem that does not rhyme and that usually consists of three lines with specific numbers of syllables. The Haiku originated in Japan.

**internment camps
(in-TURN-ment KAMPS)**
Internment camps are places where groups of people are held, especially during a war. Japanese Americans were unfairly sent to internment camps during World War II.

isolation (eye-soh-LAY-shun)
Isolation is the act of keeping someone or something apart from others. From the 1600s to the mid-1800s, Japan remained in isolation from the rest of the world.

karaoke (kar-ee-OH-kee)
Karaoke is a machine that plays music to which a person can sing along. It also records the singer's voice with the music. Karaoke is a form of Japanese entertainment that is popular with many different people. The word karaoke comes from the Japanese *kara*, which means "empty" and *oke*, short for *Okesutora*, which means "orchestra."

resentment (ri-ZENT-ment)
Resentment is the act of feeling angry about a real or imagined wrongdoing. Many Americans felt resentment toward the Japanese after the bombing of Pearl Harbor.

sawmills (SAW-milz)
Sawmills are factories that have machines for cutting logs of wood. Some Japanese immigrants on the West Coast worked in sawmills.

suburbs (SUB-erbs)
Suburbs are residential communities that are near big cities. As Japanese Americans became successful in the United States, they moved to the suburbs.

tradition (truh-DISH-un)
A tradition is a custom or belief that has been handed down through generations or within cultures. For centuries, there were very specific traditions in Japan.

For Further Information

Web Sites

Visit our homepage for lots of links about Japanese Americans:
http://www.childsworld.com/links.html

Note to Parents, Teachers, and Librarians:
We routinely verify our Web links to make sure they're safe,
active sites—so encourage your readers to check them out!

Books

Cooper, Michael L. *Fighting for Honor: Japanese Americans and World War II.* New York: Clarion, 2000.

Crilley, Mark. *Akiko and the Great Wall of Trudd.* New York: Delacorte Press, 2001.

Fremon, David K. *Japanese-American Internment in American History.* Springfield, N.J.: Enslow Publishers, 1996.

Hamanaka, Sheila. *Journey: Japanese Americans, Racism, and Renewal.* New York: Orchard Books, 1995.

Lee, Lauren. *Japanese Americans.* Tarrytown, N.Y.: Marshall Cavendish, 1996.

Takaki, Ronald. *Democracy and Race: Asian Americans and World War II.* New York: Chelsea House, 1995.

Takaki, Ronald. *Issei and Nissei: The Settling of Japanese America.* New York: Chelsea House, 1994.

Uchida, Yoshiko. *Jar of Dreams.* New York: Aladdin Paperbacks, 1993.

Places to Visit or Contact

Japanese American National Museum
369 East First Street
Los Angeles, CA 90012
213-625-0414

National Japanese American Historical Society
1684 Post Street
San Francisco, CA 94115
415-921-5007

Index